# 101 HILAR... YO MAMA JOKES

Laugh Out Loud With These Funny Yo Momma Jokes: So Bad, Even Your Mum Will Crack Up! (WITH 25+ PICTURES)

# Table of Contents

# INTRODUCTION

**First joke**: Your momma is so dumb, I saw her putting a quarter in a parking meter and waiting for a gumball to come out!

**Or how about this one:**

Your momma is so fat, when she went to KFC the girl behind the counter asked her, "What size bucket?" and your momma said, "Give me the one on the roof!"

Thank you for picking up a copy of '*101 Hilarious Yo Mama Jokes*'.

**Are you ready to crack up about Yo Mama?**

<u>Laughter is good</u> for you!

You probably already knew that. I mean, who doesn't feel good when they laugh, right?

But did you know that laughter is associated with all these health benefits?

Laughter:

- relaxes your body
- boosts your immune system
- triggers the release of feel-good hormones, such as endorphins
- protects your heart

Sound good?

Well, you have come to the right place!

**This book is jam-packed with:**

- 100+ hilarious Yo Mama jokes, and
- 25+ funny illustrations

that will have you *grin*, *LOL*, and *roar with laughter*.

So, I hope you are ready: **let's have a laugh about Yo Mama!**

# 101 HILARIOUS YO MAMA JOKES

# 1.

Your momma is so poor, when she saw the garbage truck she went running after it with a grocery list.

# 2.

Your momma is so dumb, she went back to Dunkin' Donuts to return a donut because it had a hole in it!

# 3.

Your momma is so dumb, she once opened a bag of M&M's and tried to put them in alphabetical order.

# 4.

Your momma is so dumb, when thieves broke
into her house and stole the coffee machine,
she followed them outside and yelled to them,
"Hey, you forgot the coffee!"

# 5.

Your momma is so fat, one day she saw a yellow school bus go by filled with white kids and she ran after it yelling, "TWINKIE!"

# *6.*

Your momma is so dumb, she brought a spoon to watch the Super Bowl.

# 7.

Your momma is so fat, last Christmas I took a picture of her and it's still printing now.

# *8.*

Your momma is so ugly, she forced One Direction to go another direction.

# 9.

Your momma is so dumb, I saw her put two quarters in her ears and then she thought she was listening to a 50 Cent record.

# 10.

Your momma is so fat, this morning she stepped on the scale and it said, "I need your weight girl, not your phone number."

# *11.*

Your momma is so dumb, when your family was driving in the car to Disneyland, she noticed a sign that said "Disneyland left," so she turned around to go home.

# 12.

Yo momma is so fat, when I told her to bend over and touch her feet, she said, "What are those"?

# *13.*

Your momma is so fat, when she went to the beach a giant humpback whale swam up to her and said, "We are family, even though you're bigger than me."

# *14.*

Your momma is so ugly, one day she wanted to participate in an ugly contest, but they said, "Sorry, amateurs only."

# *15.*

Your momma is so dumb, I saw her sit on the Television to watch the couch!

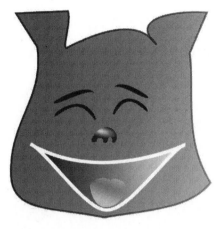

Your momma is so chubby, one day she sat on an iPod and made the iPad!

# 17.

Your momma is so fat, when she went to the pool in her black bathing suit, everyone yelled, "watch out, oil spill!"

# *18.*

Your momma is so dumb, when her phone broke down she called Taco Bell.

# *19.*

Yo momma is so poor, I stepped in a puddle the other day, when her head popped out and said, "Hey, get out of my bathtub!"

# *20.*

Your momma is so fat, when she fell in love she broke it.

# 21.

Your momma is so ugly, when she brought a cow into Tesco, one of the employees said, "Get that cow out of here," and the cow replied, "My bad, it won't happen again!"

# 22.

Your momma is so old and fat, when God created light, he told her to move out of the way.

# 23.

Your momma is so dumb, she said "These walls are not green!", when she walked into Walgreens.

# 24.

Your momma is so fat, she causes a tsunami when she sweats.

# 25.

Your momma is so fat, when she steps into an elevator, she only has to go down.

# 26.

Your momma is so fat, when she goes to check her BMI the doctor measures it in acres.

# 27.

Your momma is so old, Maria asked her to babysit Jesus.

# **28.**

Your momma is so fat, her belly button gets home 10 minutes before her.

# 29.

Your momma is so dumb, when a burglar broke into her apartment, she ran to the kitchen, touched 911 on the microwave, but couldn't find the "Call" button.

# *30.*

Your momma is so dumb, she once cancelled a hockey game because there was ice on the field.

# 31.

Your momma is so poor, when I saw her walking in the park with only one shoe on, I told her, "Hey, you're missing a shoe!" and she replied, "No, I found a shoe!"

# 32.

Your momma is so ugly, when I told her to do the robot, R2-D2 got HIV.

# **33.**

Your momma is so dumb, when she was hungry she went to the Apple Store to get an apple.

# *34.*

Your momma is so dumb, she once tried to climb Mountain Dew.

# 35.

Your momma is so fat, one half of her is in this universe, and the other half in a parallel universe.

# 36.

Your momma is so fat, nobody was laughing when she fell down, but the ground was cracking up.

# 37.

Your momma is so fat, she sat next to everybody when she went to the movie theater.

# 38.

Your momma is so dumb, when she came over to my house but didn't find me at home, she left me a voicemail by shouting in my mailbox.

# 39.

Your momma is so fat, she wakes up on both sides of the bed in the morning.

# 40.

Your momma is so dumb, when she went to the World Cup she brought tea bags!

# 41.

Your momma is so fat, she measures 36-24-36, and her right arm has the same size.

# 42.

Your momma is so old, she knew the rapper 50 Cent when he was only 25 Cent.

# 43.

Your momma is so dumb, when you were born in the hospital and she saw your cord, she exclaimed, "Oh, great, he comes with a cable!"

Yo momma is so dumb, when I told her it was chilly outside, she went to the kitchen to get a plate.

# **45.**

Your momma is so dumb, when she was applying for a job, and the application form said, "Do not write here", she wrote "Ok."

# 46.

Your momma is so dumb, she returned a puzzle to Amazon because she thought it was broken!

# 47.

Your momma is so fat, she couldn't get in or out when she went to get a burger at In and Out.

# 48.

Your momma's has so much dandruff in her hair, when she shook her head left and right, the school principal called a snow day.

# 49.

Your momma is so fat, Bill Gates declared for bankruptcy after taking her out for dinner.

# *50.*

Your momma is so ugly, she's the reason why
Sonic the Hedgehog runs like crazy.

# 51.

Your momma is so poor, when somebody accidentally stepped on her cigarette, she asked, "Hey, who turned off the heat?"

# 52.

Your momma is so fat, when she did a push-up, planet Earth went down.

# 53.

Your momma is so crusty, Pizza Hut hired her as a consultant.

# 54.

Your momma is so thin, when it rains, she can dodge the raindrops.

# 55.

Your momma is so fat, it is a long-distance call whenever she talks to herself.

# 56.

Your momma is so ugly, when she went to the beautician, it took 10 hours – and that was only for a quote!

# 57.

Your momma is so fat, when she applied to be a bus driver, they told her she was qualified to be the bus.

# 58.

Your momma is so fat, when Jabba's guard from Star Wars pushed her down into the Sarlacc pit, the pit choked to death.

# 59.

Your momma is so fat, she doesn't need an internet data plan on her phone: she is already worldwide.

# **60.**

Your momma is so fat that she got stuck when she jumped for joy!

# *61.*

Your momma is so dumb, I once saw her trying to drown a fish.

# 62.

Your mom is so black, the "check oil" light turns on when she opens the door and gets out of the car.

# 63.

Your momma is so big, when she got hit by a bus she asked, "Who threw a rock at me?"

# 64.

Your momma is so old, when she closes her eyes to relive the past, her memories are in black and white.

# 65.

Your momma is so old, when the clerk told her to act her own age, she fell down and died on the spot.

# 66.

Your momma is so fat, when she walked to Wendy's, she fell over McDonalds and landed on Burger King.

# 67.

Your momma is so fat, she is the circle of life that Elton John sang about in The Lion King.

# 68.

Your momma is so hairy, she uses a lawnmower to shave her legs.

# 69.

Your momma is so dumb, when she calls the psychic hotline for a mind reading, they charge her only half price!

# *70.*

Your momma is so old, her Bible is signed by the author.

# 71.

Your momma is so hairy, when Bigfoot saw her he stole her camera to take a snapshot of her!

# 72.

Your momma is so black, she makes Snoop Dogg look like Casper the friendly ghost.

# **73.**

Your momma is so old, when she was in high school they didn't teach history yet!

# 74.

Your momma is so ugly, she didn't just get hit with the ugly stick. They used the whole tree on her!

# 75.

Your momma is so ugly, Waldo said she is the reason he is hiding.

# 76.

Your momma is so poor, she washes her paper
coffee cups.

# 77.

Your momma is so fat, when people go for a run, they jog around her.

# 78.

Your momma is so poor, you and your family ate cereal with a fork, to save milk!

# 79.

Your momma is so fat, when she went for a swim, Columbus claimed her for new land.

# *80.*

Your momma is so fat, they gave her a group discount when she went to eat at Sizzler.

# *81.*

Your momma is so fat, her shadow broke the sidewalk in two.

# 82.

Your momma is so fat, when she did a bungee
jump, she ended up all the way in Hell.

# *83.*

Your momma and the sun have a lot in common: they're huge, round, and your eyes start to hurt looking at it.

# *84.*

Your momma is so dumb, she thought she could freeze time by putting her watch in the fridge!

# 85.

Your mom is so ugly, when she put on her make-up, it jumped off!

# 86.

Your momma is so hairy, when she lifted her armpit, Guns 'n' Roses busted through the door and started to play "Welcome to the Jungle."

# *87.*

Your momma is so ugly, that if they would measure one's ugliness bricks, they would call her the Great Wall of China.

# *88.*

Your momma is so old, her left boob fell off when I put my hand on her back.

# 89.

Your momma is so dumb, she told me sharks smoke seaweed.

# 90.

Your momma is so fat, Earth tilted when she fell off the couch.

# 91.

Your momma is so fat, when the photographer pointed the camera at her and said "Cheese", she asked, "Where?"

# 92.

Your momma is so fat, each time she completes a 360° turn, it is her birthday.

# 93.

Your momma is so dumb, she sold her Mustang to get money for gas.

# 94.

Your momma is so fat, I feel like insulting her,
but I'm from India, and cows are sacred in my
country.

# 95.

Your momma is so dumb, she challenged a Ford Focus to a staring contest.

# 96.

Your momma is so dumb, when she watched the CBS show '60 Minutes', it took her 2 hours.

# 97.

Your momma is so poor, she panicked when we talked about 'the Last Supper', because she thought she had run out of food stamps.

# 98.

Your momma is so black, when I went to Facebook and clicked on her profile picture, I thought my laptop crashed.

# 99.

Your momma is so dumb, she bought tickets to go see X-Box perform Live.

# *100.*

Your momma is so dumb, when you asked a color television for your 16th birthday, she replied, "Which color would you like, sweetie?"

# 101.

Your momma is so tall, she hit Jesus in the face when she did a salto.

# *BONUS JOKES*

*This is a bonus chapter from my book '101 HILARIOUS DUMB BLONDE JOKES.'*

*Enjoy!*

\*\*\*

# *1.*

One day, a blonde went to a pizzeria and ordered a pizza. The waitress asked if she wanted her pizza cut into six or twelve pieces. "Six", the blonde replied, "You don't really think I eat twelve, do you?!"

# 2.

A brunette, a blonde and a redhead got lost on a hike in the desert. After walking for hours, they stumbled upon a lamp, half buried in the sand. As they rubbed it, a genie popped out! He said: "I will grant each of you one wish."

Excited, the redhead said: "I wish to be back home". And poof!, the next moment she found herself back in her home.

Next, the brunette said: "I wish to be with my family, at home". Poof!, she was also transported back home immediately, surrounded by her loved ones.

Then the blonde said: "I wish my friends were here."

# 3.

When going for a walk, two blondes fell down a deep and dark hole. After checking in with each other, one blonde said, "It is really dark in here, right?" To which the other blonde replied, "I honestly don't know, I can't see anything!"

# 4.

Q: Why can't a blonde dial 911?

A: She gets stuck trying to find eleven.

# 5.

A brunette, a blonde and a redhead found themselves trapped on an island. They decided their only option for survival was to try to swim to the nearest shore, 40 miles away.

The brunette went first. She swam 20 miles, but then was so exhausted that she drowned.

The redhead swam 25 miles, but then also drowned.

Finally, the blonde swam 35 miles, but when she got tired, she swam back.

# 6.

Q: How do you confuse a blonde?

A: Tell to her sit in the corner, after putting her in a circle.

# 7.

In the 19th century, a brunette, a redhead, and a blonde are on death row. They are about to be executed by a firing squad.

The guards start with the brunette. When she is asked if she has any last request, she says: "No." The guards point their guns at her, when the captain shouts: "Ready. Aim..." But then, suddenly, the brunette screams, "Tornado!" As everyone is freaking out, looking for shelter, the brunette escapes.

Next, the guards put the redhead against the wall. She also says "No" when she is asked if she has a last request. The captain shouts "Ready. Aim...", and then the redhead yells "Earthquake!" Again, the guards are freaking out, running all over the place, and in the commotion, the redhead is able to escape.

All this time, the blonde has been paying attention. And she knows what to do now. The guards put her against the wall. When asked, she says she doesn't have any final requests. The captain says:

bring her forward, and the executioner asks if she has any last requests. She also says no, and the executioner yells "Ready. Aim..."

The blonde screams, "Fire!"

# *8.*

Q: Why does it take hours to build a blonde snowman?

A: Because, unlike a regular snowman, you need to hollow out the head.

# 9.

One day, three blondes went on a walk in the woods. After a few hours, they spotted some tracks.

The first blonde said, excited: "Look, it's bear tracks!"

The second blonde replied, "No, those are deer tracks".

Before the third blonde was able to share her opinion, the blondes got hit by a train...

# *10.*

Q: What do you call a blonde with a high IQ?

A: A golden retriever.

# 11.

200 blondes came together in Los Angeles, intent on showing the people that blondes can be smart. They said to the people passing by: "You can ask us anything you want! Anything. We will show you we're smarter than you think."

A passer-by took them up on their offer. He chose one blonde from the group, and asked her the first question, surrounded by the other 199 blondes.

"Who is the president of the United States?" The blonde said: "Michael Jordan?" "I'm sorry, that's not correct," the man said. The other blondes then chanted: "Please let her try again!"

The man then asked: "What's the color of grass?" The blonde said: "Blue?". "No, it's green", the man responded. The group of blondes began shouting again: "Let her try again!"

The man was running out of patience, and said: "I'll give her one more chance, but this is the last question! How many corners does a triangle have?" The blonde responded: "Three?"

"Please let her try again!", the group of blondes yelled...

*** 

*This is the end of this bonus chapter.*

*Want to continue reading?*

*Then go to Amazon and search for "101 Hilarious Dumb Blonde Jokes"*

*Hope to see you there!*

# DID YOU LIKE THIS BOOK?

If you enjoyed this book, I would like to ask you for a favor. Please leave a review on Amazon!

Reviews are the lifeblood of independent authors. I know, you're short on time. But I would really appreciate even just a few sentences!

Your voice is important for this book to reach as many people as possible.

You can find the book by going to Amazon and:

- Checking your purchases, or
- Searching for "101 Hilarious Yo Mama Jokes"

The more reviews this book gets, the more people will be able to find it and have a good laugh with these funny jokes!

***

IF YOU DID NOT LIKE THIS BOOK, THEN PLEASE TELL ME! You can email me at feedback@semsoli.com, to share with me what you did not like.

Perhaps I can change it.

A book does not have to be stagnant, in today's world. With feedback from readers like yourself, I can improve the book. So, you can impact the quality of this book, and I welcome your feedback. Help make this book better for everyone!

Thank you again for reading this book: I hope you had a good laugh!